Mayors

by Shannon Knudsen
photographs by Stephen G. Donaldson

Lerner Publications Company • Minneapolis

Lerner Publications Company
A division of Lerner Publishing Group
241 First Avenue North
Minneapolis, MN 55401 U.S.A.

Website address: www.lernerbooks.com

Library of Congress Cataloging-in-Publication Data

Knudsen, Shannon, 1971–
    Mayors / by Shannon Knudsen ; photographs by
Stephen G. Donaldson.
        p.   cm. – (Pull ahead books)
    Includes index.
    ISBN–13: 978–0–8225–2829–6 (lib. bdg. : alk. paper)
    ISBN–10: 0–8225–2829–0 (lib. bdg. : alk. paper)
    1. Mayors–United States–Juvenile literature.
I. Donaldson, Stephen G. II. Title. III. Series.
JS346.K68 2006
352.23'216'0973–dc22   2005003210

Manufactured in the United States of America
1 2 3 4 5 6 – JR – 11 10 09 08 07 06

Who is the leader of your **community**?

Many communities have a leader called
a **mayor**. Mayors work to make their
communities better places to live.

Mayors in different communities do different jobs.

What are some jobs that mayors do?

Some mayors run groups of workers called **departments**. Each department helps the community in different ways. The police department fights crime.

The fire department fights fires. It
rescues people from burning buildings.

Some mayors also run the community's **transportation**. Buses, trains, and subways take people where they need to go.

This community needs more homes.
Where should they be built? The mayor
talks with workers in the housing
department to find out.

Mayors work to make schools better. Mayors talk to principals, teachers, and kids about how to help kids learn.

Mayors also help make laws for their community. This mayor is meeting with a group called the **city council**.

The council talks about new laws.
It decides how to spend the community's
money. Where does the money
come from?

Part of the money comes from the mayor!
Mayors do not give the money
themselves. They visit their state
government to ask for money
for the community.

Mayors help make a community a nicer place to live. This mayor is visiting with senior citizens.

Important visitors have come to this city.
The mayor shows them around town.

This mayor is honoring people who have helped the community. The mayor gives awards for jobs well done.

Mayors help people celebrate too.

A mayor might attend a special
school event.

Here is a parade. The mayor leads the way!

This mayor leads a wedding. A happy couple will soon be married.

How is a person chosen to do this important job? How does someone become a mayor?

In most communities, the mayor is chosen by the adults who live there. The people who run for mayor are called **candidates**.

Candidates make speeches. They tell people their ideas about how to run the community.

Candidates also meet people and talk with them. Sometimes candidates meet to talk about how their ideas are different.

It is **election** day! Adults **vote** for the person they want to become the mayor. Then the votes are counted.

The candidate who gets the most votes
wins the election. That candidate
becomes the new mayor.

Mayors lead our communities in
many ways.

Someday you can help choose your mayor by voting. Maybe you will run for mayor yourself!

Facts about Mayors

■ Some mayors have a special power called a veto. A mayor can veto a law made by the city council. That means the law will not be carried out. But some city councils can undo a veto if enough members vote against it.

■ How does one mayor run all the departments in a community? The mayor chooses a person to run each department. Those people carry out the mayor's orders.

■ Some communities have no mayor. They are run by a group called a board or a council, or by a city manager who is chosen by the board.

Mayors through History

Cities have not always been led by mayors. In many places, city leaders were chosen by a king, a governor, or another powerful person. People did not have a choice about who led their city. This is still true in parts of the world.

■ Susanna Salter was the first woman mayor in the United States. She was elected mayor of Argonia, Kansas, in 1887.

■ The first woman mayor of a large city in the United States was Bertha K. Landes. She became mayor of Seattle, Washington, in 1926.

■ One of the youngest mayors of a large city in the United States is Kwame Kilpatrick. He became the mayor of Detroit, Michigan, in 2001 at the age of 31.

More about Mayors

Check out these websites to find out more about mayors. Or visit a town hall or city hall and see if you can talk to the mayor there.

Websites

City of Atlanta (Georgia) Online: Meet the Mayor
http://www.atlantaga.gov/Mayor/Meet.aspx

City of Boston (Massachusetts) Mayor's Office
http://www.cityofboston.gov/mayor/default.asp

City of Houston (Texas) Mayor's Office
http://www.houstontx.gov/mayor/index.html

City of Los Angeles (California) Office of the Mayor
http://www.lacity.org/mayor/

City of Minneapolis (Minnesota) Office of the Mayor
http://www.ci.minneapolis.mn.us/mayor/

Glossary

candidates: people who try to win a government job

city council: a group that makes laws for a city

community: a group of people who live in the same city, town, or neighborhood. People in the same community usually share the same fire department, schools, libraries, and other helpful places.

departments: groups of workers who try to meet a community's needs

election: a way of choosing a person for a government job. Each person votes for someone to get the job. Whoever gets the most votes wins the job.

mayor: a community's leader

rescues: saves from harm or danger

transportation: ways of getting from place to place

vote: to choose a person for a government job

Index

awards, 16

candidates, 21–23, 25
city council, 11–12, 28
community, 3–5, 6, 8, 9,
    11, 12, 13, 14,16, 26,
    28

departments, 6–7, 28

election day, 24

fire department, 7

housing department, 9

laws, 11–12, 28

money, 12–13

parade, 18
police department, 6

schools, 10, 17, 27

transportation, 8

wedding, 19

Photo Acknowledgments

Additional photographs courtesy of: © Alex Wong/Getty Images, p. 12; © Todd Strand/Independent Picture Service, pp. 18, 21, 23; © Erik S. Lesser/Getty Images, p. 25; © PEMCO - Webster & Stevens Collection; Museum of History and Industry, Seattle/CORBIS, p. 29.